MACHINES AT WORK >>>

Planes and Helicopters

Clive Gifford

🌳 Crabtree Publishing Company
www.crabtreebooks.com

D1455493

Crabtree Publishing Company
www.crabtreebooks.com
1-800-387-7650

PMB 59051, 350 Fifth Ave.   616 Welland Ave.
59th Floor,   St. Catharines, ON
New York, NY 10118   L2M 5V6

Published by Crabtree Publishing in 2013

Author: Clive Gifford
Editors: Nicola Edwards, Adrianna Morganelli
Proofreaders: Wendy Scavuzzo, Crystal Sikkens
Designer: Elaine Wilkinson
Picture Researcher: Clive Gifford
**Production coordinator and
    Prepress technician**: Ken Wright
Print coordinator: Katherine Berti

To find out about the author, visit his website:
www.clivegifford.co.uk

First published in 2012 by Wayland
(A division of Hachette Children's Books)
Copyright © Wayland 2012

Printed in Hong Kong/ 092012/BK20120629

Picture acknowledgements:
The author and publisher would like to thank the
following agencies and people for allowing these
pictures to be reproduced:
Cover (main) ssuaphotos / Shutterstock.com,
(inset) Balazs Toth / Shutterstock.com; title
page Steve Mann / Shutterstock.com, p3 Sascha
Hahn / Shutterstock.com; p4 (t) Christopher
Parypa / Shutterstock.com, (b) Robert Crum /
Shutterstock.com; p5 Natali Glado / Shutterstock.
com; p6 Pablo Scapinachis / Shutterstock.
com; p7 (t) Robert Rozbora / Shutterstock.
com, (b) karamysh / Shutterstock.com; p8
Sascha Hahn / Shutterstock.com; p9 (t) Eugene
Berman / Shutterstock.com, (b) Khafizov Ivan
Harisovich / Shutterstock.com; p10 (l) David
Acosta Allely / Shutterstock.com, (r) courtesy of
AgustaWestland; p11 jakelv7500 / Shutterstock.
com; p12 Carlos E. Santa Maria / Shutterstock.
com; p13 (t) iStock © Simon Parker, (b) Michael
G Smith / Shutterstock.com; p14 (l) Maurizio
Milanesio / Shutterstock.com, (r) David Fowler
/ Shutterstock.com; p15 dvande / Shutterstock.
com; p16 Steve Mann / Shutterstock.com; p17
(t) Louise Cukrov / Shutterstock.com, (b) R
McIntyre / Shutterstock.com; p18 Andrej Poi
/ Shutterstock.com; p19 (t) Maria Hetting /
Shutterstock.com, (b) Steve Mann / Shutterstock.
com; p20 iStock © Eric Gevaert; p21 (t)
Remzi / Shutterstock.com (b) Losevsky Pavel
/ Shutterstock.com; p23 Christopher Parypa /
Shutterstock.com; p24 Balazs Toth /
Shutterstock.com

**Library and Archives Canada
Cataloguing in Publication**

CIP available at Library and Archives Canada

**Library of Congress
Cataloging-in-Publication Data**

CIP available at Library of Congress

Contents

Flying machines at work

Planes and helicopters are flying machines. They leave the ground and fly high through the air, carrying people and **cargo** from place to place.

A plane takes off from an airport with more than 100 passengers on board.

Jet engines

ZOOM IN

The front area of a plane is called the **cockpit**. This is where the pilot, or driver, sits and operates the controls of the plane.

Planes and helicopters are used for many different jobs, from carrying airmail packages and taking aerial photographs to spraying crops in farm fields and rescuing climbers trapped on mountainsides.

Tail

Wings help lift the aircraft off the ground and keep it in the air

Rotor blades spin, lifting helicopter into air

Cockpit where pilot sits

A small helicopter takes off from the ground. Helicopters can fly straight up into the air.

Tail

Landing skids

Taking off

Planes and helicopters are very heavy machines. They need to create a force called **lift** to help them rise into the air when they **take off**. A plane's wings and a helicopter's rotor blades are the parts that create lift.

A large airplane takes off. Its four engines provide the thrust to move it forward, while its large wings generate plenty of lift.

A wing is curved on top and flatter along the bottom. This is called an airfoil shape. When a wing moves forward, air flows over and under it at different speeds. This helps create lift. A helicopter rotor blade has an airfoil shape, just like a plane's wing.

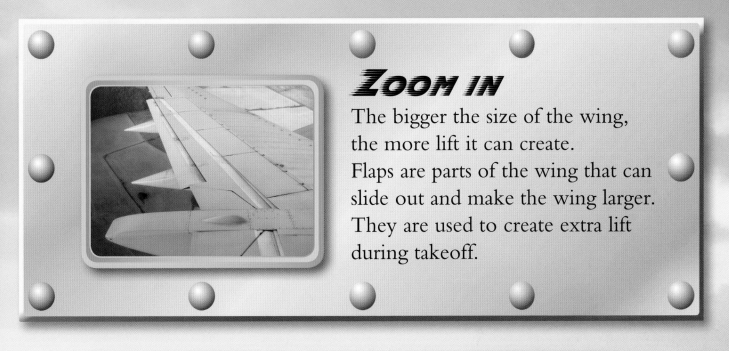

ZOOM IN

The bigger the size of the wing, the more lift it can create. Flaps are parts of the wing that can slide out and make the wing larger. They are used to create extra lift during takeoff.

A small helicopter takes off from a patch of grass at an airport. As the rotor blades swoop through the air, they create lift.

Moving forward

Engines provide the power to move planes forward through the air. Some planes can travel very long distances and reach very high speeds, far faster than other types of transportation.

This military plane is powered by two jet engines.

FAST FACT

The SR-71 Blackbird is the fastest jet plane ever. It can reach speeds of over 1,864 miles per hour (3,000 kilometers per hour)—three times the speed of a regular jet airliner.

Hot gases leave the engines at the rear

Cockpit holds the pilot and copilot

Jet engines are used to power many large airplanes and fast military planes. Other planes use **propellers**. Propellers are long, thin blades that are turned by an engine and pull the plane through the air.

This C-130 Hercules plane has four engines, each spinning a propeller. This plane is used by the U.S. Coast Guard to patrol coastlines, carry cargo, and perform rescue operations.

ZOOM IN

Jet engines suck in air and mix it with fuel before setting the mixture on fire. The burning mixture creates gases that expand out of the back of the engine, pushing the plane forward.

How do helicopters fly?

Helicopters are amazing flying machines that can take off straight upward. Instead of fixed wings, a helicopter uses long, thin, moving blades called rotors.

Rotor blades spin

Cockpit where the pilot sits

Engine underneath this panel turns the rotor blades at high speed

The pilot uses controls to spin the rotor blades faster to make the helicopter climb upward, or slower so that it travels downward.

The pilot of this helicopter has tilted the rotors forward so that they push some air backward. This thrusts the helicopter forward.

ZOOM IN

At the back of a helicopter, a small set of rotors spins in the tail. These tail rotors move the helicopter to the right and left.

The helicopter's engine spins the rotor blades quickly. As they slice through the air, they create enough lift to raise the helicopter up.

Tail rotor

I-PTFT

These long flat bars are called skids

In the cockpit

Pilots sit and control planes and helicopters from the cockpit. There are a lot of controls to use and screens and dials to check. They also have a radio system for communicating with airports and other aircraft.

Navigation display

Engine indicators

Engine throttles

Control column

The **instrument panel** of an airplane is packed with controls and instruments. These give the pilot information about the plane and show how all of its parts are functioning.

In large planes, such as a passenger airplane, a copilot sits alongside the pilot in the cockpit. The copilot helps with many tasks and can take over from the pilot to fly the plane at any time.

ZOOM IN

This cockpit instrument shows the pilot whether the plane is flying level and whether it is climbing (flying upward) or descending (flying downward).

A plane flies past an airport's air traffic control tower. Controllers inside the tower organize the order in which planes take off and land at an airport. They use radios to talk to the pilots.

Steering through the sky

Pilots steer planes or helicopters from the cockpit using a yoke (steering wheel) or a control column (joystick). When pilots are flying from place to place, they use the cockpit instruments to find their way.

This helicopter pilot is flying using a control column, which is a lot like a computer game joystick.

Panels on the wings and tail of a plane can be moved up or down or from side to side. These panels are called **ailerons**. They help to direct the movement of the air around the plane and keep the plane moving in one direction.

Tail

Ailerons in the wing can tilt up or down to help the plane turn

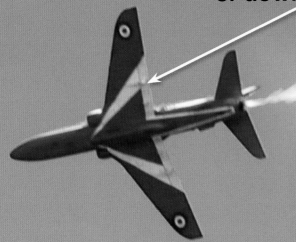

These planes are flying in an **air show** to entertain a crowd. The pilots can make their planes roll, dive down sharply toward the ground, or fly in a loop or large circle in the sky.

tailplane

rudder

elevators

ZOOM IN

The hinged rear part of the tail is called the **rudder**. It helps the plane steer right and left. **Elevators** on the tailplane are hinged flaps that help the plane move up or down.

Landing

Most planes land on a **runway** using their **landing gear**. These are sets of wheels that are lowered for landing and raised up into the body of the plane during the flight.

FAST FACT

A Boeing 777 airplane lands at a speed of 152 to177 mph (245 to 285 km/h) and needs around 5,577 feet (1,700 m) of runway to come to a stop safely.

This plane's landing gear has ten wheels covered in rubber tires. The wheels have to support the weight of the airplane when it is on the ground.

ZOOM IN

To land a helicopter, the pilot slows the speed of the rotor blades. This creates less lifting force and allows the helicopter to travel gently downward.

Not all planes land on wheels. Seaplanes take off and land on water. They have large floats, or pontoons that allow it to float on water. In snowy locations, planes and helicopters may be fitted with skis or skids to land on instead of wheels.

This Twin Otter seaplane lands in the Indian Ocean. Instead of wheels, the plane uses large floats that allow it to sit on top of the water when it lands.

Helicopters at work

Helicopters can take off straight upward, fly forward, and even **hover** in midair. This makes them very useful for many different jobs. For example, helicopters can reach and rescue injured climbers on a mountainside.

This helicopter hovers in midair as a crew member travels down on a strong cable to rescue a person in the ocean. The two people will then be lifted back up into the helicopter by the cable.

Helicopters are good at flying to hard-to-reach places. Since they can take off straight upward, they do not need a long runway. Instead, they can fly to and from a **helipad** or a small area of ground. Helipads can be found on ships and on the roof tops of tall city buildings.

ZOOM IN

This helipad is on an oil rig in the middle of the sea. Helicopters can move workers and supplies to and from the rig.

This Chinook helicopter has two pairs of rotor blades. It can lift heavy loads, such as this jeep and trailer, and fly them to another location.

Carrying passengers

Some planes carry enormous loads through the air. Airplanes fly hundreds of passengers and their **luggage** between airports all over the world. A plane's **hold** is where passengers' luggage and other cargo, such as airmail parcels, are stored.

Hold

An airplane is unloaded at an airport. The plane needs to be cleaned and refueled then loaded with new passengers and their luggage before it makes another flight.

FAST FACT

The largest plane in the world is the Airbus A380. It can carry up to 853 passengers.

ZOOM IN

Inside the airplane, seats are placed in rows separated by walkways called aisles. Passengers can store small bags, called carry-on luggage, in overhead storage compartments.

A row of airplanes, each parked at a separate gate at an airport. The tunnels are passenger walkways that connect the planes to the airport buildings.

Quiz

How much have you found out about how planes and helicopters work? Try this short quiz!

1. Which person controls and flies a plane or helicopter?
a) air traffic controller
b) pilot
c) engineer

2. Which part of a plane helps it to fly higher or lower?
a) elevators
b) rudder
c) artificial horizon

3. What type of plane can take off and land on water?
a) ski plane
b) seaplane
c) Boeing 747

4. What does a helicopter have in instead of fixed wings?
a) rotor blades
b) flaps
c) propellers

5. What force do plane wings create when the plane moves forward?
a) friction
b) thrust
c) lift

6. What is the world's largest plane?
a) Boeing 747
b) Airbus A380
c) Boeing 777

7. What part of a helicopter helps it steer to the left or right?
a) tail rotor
b) skids
c) main rotor

8. Where is luggage and cargo stored in a plane?
a) cockpit
b) wings
c) hold

Answers: 1.b, 2.a, 3.b, 4.a, 5.c, 6.b, 7.a, 8.c

Glossary

air show Spectacular stunts, such as loops and rolls, usually performed by special planes to thrill spectators

ailerons Movable edges of the wings that can tilt up or down to help a plane turn

cargo Materials or goods carried on a plane, train, ship, or truck

cockpit The part of the plane that contains the plane's controls and where the pilot sits

copilot A trained pilot who sits beside or behind the pilot and can take over the controls when necessary

elevators Flaps on the tailplane that can move to help the plane climb higher into the air or fly lower

helipad A small area, usually marked with the letter **H**, from which helicopters take off and land

hold The part of a plane where luggage and cargo is stored

hover To stay suspended in one spot in the air

instrument panel The control panel in the cockpit of an aircraft

landing gear The parts of a plane that touch the ground or water when it lands

lift An upward force created by a plane's wings or a helicopter's rotor blades

luggage The suitcases, backpacks, and other passenger bags carried on planes

propeller Turning blades that help thrust a plane forward through the air

rotor Long, thin blades turned by a helicopter's engine to create lift

rudder A movable flap in a plane's tail that helps it steer

runway A strip of level ground, usually covered in a smooth surface, from which planes take off and land

take off To leave the ground and start flying through the air

Further Information

Books

On The Go: Planes, David and Penny Glover, Wayland, 2009
The World's Most Dangerous Jobs: Apache Helicopter Pilots, Antony Loveless,
Crabtree Publishing 2010
Hovering Helicopters, Molly Aloian, Crabtree Publishing, 2010

Websites

WayBack: Flight: http://pbskids.org/wayback/flight/
*This PBS site contains a lot of fascinating information about flight through
the ages. It includes the U.S. Mail service, the Wright brothers, and barnstormers.
There are a lot of pictures, as well as interesting facts and information.*

The Dynamics of Airplane Flight: http://inventors.about.com/library/inventors/
blairplanedynamics.htm
*A detailed webpage about airplane flight that covers air flow, lift, control, parts of the plane, and the forces that
act on a plane.*

The National Air and Space Museum: The Wright Brothers & The Invention of the Aerial Age:
http://airandspace.si.edu/wrightbrothers/
This website contains several enlargeable photographs of the Wright brothers' planes and a brief history of each.

Index